TAKE CONTROL

OF WHAT'S CONTROLLING YOU

A Guide to Personal Freedom

TAKE CONTROL

OF WHAT'S
CONTROLLING
YOU

A Guide to Personal Freedom

Stephen Arterburn
and Debra Cherry

INTEGRITY
HOUSE™
Nashville, Tennessee

Experience the Presence of God

Copyright © 2006 by Stephen Arterburn

Published by Integrity Publishers, a division of Integrity Media, Inc., 660 Bakers Bridge Avenue, Suite 200, Franklin, TN 37067.

Stephen Arterburn published in association with Alive Communications, 7680 Goddard Street, Suite 200, Colorado Springs, Colorado 80920.

Debra Cherry published in association with Yates & Yates, LLP, Literary Agents, Orange, California.

Scripture taken from the HOLY BIBLE, NEW INTERNATIONAL VERSION®. NIV®. Copyright ©1973, 1978, 1984 by International Bible Society. Used by permission of Zondervan. All rights reserved.

Cover Design: The Designworks Group

Interior Design: Kimberly Sagmiller, VisibilityCreative.com

ISBN 10: 1-59145-478-6
ISBN 13: 978-1-59145-478-6

06 07 08 09 LBM 9 8 7 6 5 4 3 2 1

CONTENTS

INTRODUCTION
Yes, You *Can* Take Control!

Alcohol. Power. Money. Food. Sex. Shopping. Gambling. All are capable of causing normal appetites to become full-blown addictions. More than twenty-five years ago, I (Steve) started working with people whose appetites were out of control. Desire had literally taken over and caused ruin in their lives.

I have been exactly where they were. I remember what life was like out of control and how I was barely hopeful of a life beyond mere survival. My first struggle was with food. Enough was never enough. My favorite women were Sara Lee, Little Debbie, Aunt Jemima, and Mrs. Butterworth. Given a chance, I would have become a lover to any of them. And that was my other problem appetite. Sex became a soothing, satisfying fix for me. I was promiscuous and loved to be loved. But no woman could fill the emptiness I felt inside. Not even the baby I created with one filled that void. And the subsequent abortion I paid for intensified the appetites of my heart.

Food and sex couldn't heal what was wrong. So

when I started working with people whose appetites were out of control, like mine, I was actually working for me. I met others who were on the road to recovery and regaining control of their lives. These successful people were learning how to be conquered by nothing because they were finding out how to crave nothing. Their humility and gratitude regarding their victory was intriguing and palpable. I wanted to be like them; I wanted to possess their wisdom and be in possession of myself.

So I set out on a journey to understand what I had to do to get my appetites under control. Along the way I learned something amazing: Every human being has an inborn desire to know God, but our personal and selfish wants get in the way. Our desire for knowledge of our Creator is taken hostage, and we find ourselves captured instead by appetites for foods, feelings, or experiences. We can identify with the words of the apostle Paul in Romans 7:15 and following: "I do not understand what I do. For what I want to do I do not do, but what I hate I do. . . . For I have the desire to do what is good, but I cannot carry it out. . . . Now if I do what I do not want to do, it is no longer I who do it, but it is sin living in me that does it."

Paul is talking about sin in the theological sense. Adam and Eve's desires were in perfect harmony with God and His creation. But with the Fall, sin came into the world and has ever since caused mankind's appetites to become attached—and even enslaved—to various ungodly behaviors, material possessions, and even people.

When I fully understood this reality, I realized that my choices to satisfy my various problem appetites were symptomatic of my ongoing, willful rebelliousness against God. God gave me these appetites. I am supposed to live as He intended and to enjoy Him. However, when I let my appetites get out of balance and allowed them to take priority in my life, God became distant and my behavior less Christlike.

Before now you may not have given much thought to what drives your life and why certain behaviors seem out of control—or that there is a connection between your personal addictions and your walk with the Lord. If so, you are not alone. I am one such example. When I realized I couldn't get my appetites under control on my own strength, I started down the road to healing. After I surrendered my considerable burdens to the God who created me and admitted that fixing myself was beyond my capabilities, God brought my appetites back under control.

Perhaps you are in the same place I was, unsure of how to begin a journey of healing from out-of-control appetites. If so, this is the book for you. This journey won't be quick, and it won't be easy. Change requires perseverance, even when our circumstances are painful and the journey takes a long time.

Think of this book as a roadmap for the journey to get your appetites and desires back on track. Your ten-chapter journey through these pages will lead you through ten life-liberating steps for taking control of the controlling appetites in your life. Take time to internalize one step at a time, then move on to the next. By the end of this book, you will be well on your way to the life of freedom you have longed for.

By picking up this book, you have demonstrated your desire to seek help and ultimately find healing. We want the life God meant you to live to be a reality, and we are so glad you chose this book as a resource to get there. Let us now start on the road to taking control of our appetites. It's a journey that will set you free.

1

ENJOY LIFE TO THE FULLEST

The greatest thing about man is his ability to transcend himself, his ancestry and his environment and to become what he dreams of being.
Tully C. Knoles

As unique and special as each person is, all of us share a single trait. At the core of our being, we are all searching to experience fulfillment. Though that desire may drive some of us to look in one place while others choose a different route, the fact remains that we are all on the same journey. For most of us, our quest for fulfillment is a search to love and be loved, to have meaning and purpose, and to be satisfied with who we are.

We have been formed in the image of God with this innate need to become complete, whole, satisfied. Try as we may, we cannot escape this desire because God made us this way. So even though we might not know exactly what we are searching for, we can't stop trying to satisfy this inner void.

We spend much of our time trying to meet our longing for fulfillment. Our search for fulfillment drives us forward and motivates us to meet our needs and fulfill our wants. The appetites we have for those things that are necessary for our physical, emotional, and spiritual survival help fill that void.

No matter how many stories we hear about certain things in life not bringing fulfillment, we still develop strong appetites for those very things. Some choose to go after money, working and living as if their life depended on attaining wealth. Every decision, and for some, each waking moment, is driven by an appetite for more and more money.

Others struggle with an appetite for power. It matters little whether it is a mother who insists on controlling every aspect of her children's lives or a corporate executive who cannot function unless he micromanages every detail and every decision he can possibly control. Both have an appetite for total control, which, even if they were to attain it, will never bring fulfillment. Quite the opposite, this appetite produces great frustration because much of what happens is beyond our pathetically short reach.

Your natural appetites to be loved and secure are not wrong in and of themselves, but how you go about fulfilling those appetites can very quickly turn ugly if you are not careful. The natural appetite for companionship cannot be fulfilled with prostitution, pornography, or sleeping with another person only for your pleasure. These are wrong choices for a normal, God-given appetite that, when fulfilled correctly, brings men and women together to marry, have families, and love one another.

This appetite for intimacy, like all the other appetites God has given us, can direct us to experience physical health, loving relationships, and contentment or illness, isolation, and despair, depending on how we fulfill it. Not surprisingly, how you fulfill your appetites needs to be aligned with what God has ordained in His Word.

You Were Created for a Purpose

Let's look at what Scripture has to say about how

we are made. Psalm 139:13–14 declares, "For you created my inmost being; you knit me together in my mother's womb. I praise you because I am fearfully and wonderfully made; your works are wonderful." We are the work of God's hands, His handmade treasures. When something is handmade, there are no two models that are exactly alike. God took the time to knit me together in my mother's womb. And He knit you together too. Picture yourself as part of that concept. Imagine being uniquely planned, formed, and knit together by the Creator of our entire universe.

As unique individuals, we are knit together with our own set of likes, dislikes, desires, talents, and skills that work together to help us accomplish what God had in mind when He made us. Because He knew His plans for you, He placed inside you all the talents, skills, and even appetites and desires that you would need to accomplish just what He had in mind. You are unique and created with a unique purpose; therefore, your appetites and desires are unique.

All of this is to say that the things that will fulfill our appetites are going to be diverse and varied from one person to the next. Some of us have stronger appetites in one area or another, while other people may have no desire at all for what we do. Whatever you do will reflect your distinctive set of appetites and desires, whether it be:

- the career you choose,
- the way you spend your money,
- how often you want sex and what kind of sex you want,
- the types of friends you build relationships with,
- the amount of champagne you drink at a party, or
- how you prioritize your activities.

You don't need to compare yourself to anyone else to determine whether what you are doing is right. You only need to seek God and compare your actions with His plan for your life. And just so you know, if you are seeking Him first, then your appetites will be fulfilled in ways that glorify God and benefit you and others.

What Are Your Appetites?

An appetite is any strong desire we have to fill a specific

need, such as the craving for food, sex, power, pleasure, work, companionship, wisdom, or even God. Appetite is something everyone experiences on a daily basis in one form or another. It can also be our internal need to fill an emotional or spiritual void. This appetite to fill ourselves with any of the many facets of our lives is what drives us to search outside of ourselves for that missing piece.

Appetites are essential to our physical, emotional, and spiritual survival. When hungry, the body craves food, and when thirsty, the body craves water. When you hold your breath, you crave oxygen. Were it not for these cravings motivating us to act, we would not survive. If you never felt cravings for food, you would never eat and you would die.

Our appetites motivate us to seek fulfillment, but they must be managed or they will lead us into a world of regret and tremendous emotional pain. When an appetite intended to help us survive is managed incorrectly, it may become a deadly trap. Until we give ourselves and our appetites completely over to God, we will remain trapped.

The world offers a smorgasbord of options to fill

whatever void might be present in our life. What we choose is up to us. As you know, there are healthy and unhealthy means of filling our appetites; what we choose makes a difference in our personal sense of happiness and satisfaction. Of course what we should want is to pick the healthiest choice available to fulfill our need.

If you are not feeling fulfilled, it is very likely that one of your appetites is not being fed. The longer an appetite goes unattended, the stronger it becomes. It drives us harder and faster to be satisfied. Appetites do not like to be ignored. So what happens when a person has an unsatisfied desire and cannot satisfy his needs? Eventually that person will go in search of any means, healthy or otherwise, to alleviate that need.

Take for example the man who has felt unloved all his life. He has searched for fulfillment in adult relationships but has only experienced additional rejection and hurt. His appetite for companionship continues to grow stronger, and his search for relief from the pain becomes more and more desperate. He eventually starts seeking relationships with total strangers that may last only a few hours or sometimes only a few minutes. Yet he experiences a brief lull in the constant drone of that unfulfilled appetite.

To the person who is desperate to satisfy an unsatisfied appetite, even an unhealthy, temporary fix seems better than nothing. But we know this is a lie. When we settle for unhealthy and unfulfilling imitations of what we really desire, our appetites can begin to rage out of our control and start controlling us. We will turn to sources of satisfaction that will eventually turn on us and force us either to give up altogether or to overindulge until the bitter end.

Begin Your Journey

As you begin your journey to a better understanding of your appetites, we pray you will learn that with God's provision you can take control of whatever controls you. This may seem impossible. You don't want to "just try harder" one more time. Friend, you don't have to. The reason you are still struggling with your appetite is because you know that trying harder just does not work. What does work is surrendering your problem to God. You begin the journey to recovery when you admit you can't fix your appetites on your own. Keep in mind that God never expected you to. We challenge you to start evaluating your life and appetites right now. Take three minutes to answer these four questions. You don't have to write an essay—just be honest with yourself and jot down your findings.

1. What do you naturally have a strong appetite for?

2. How are you feeding that appetite?

3. Is what you are choosing satisfying and healthy for you? If not, what are you using to satisfy yourself?

4. Follow your choices down the road they are leading you on. How far will you go down that other road to satisfy that appetite?

If this self-evaluation leads you to realize that your appetites are not being satisfied in healthy ways and are in fact controlling you, these next two questions are for you.

1. Are you ready to give up your unhealthy appetites?

2. Are you willing to learn to fill your healthy appetites as God intended them to be filled?

We are willing to share with you from the foundation of God's Word what it will take to control what's controlling you. In the next chapter we look at God's plan for our appetites right from the beginning.

A MOMENT TO REFLECT

1. What happens when a person has an unsatisfied desire and cannot fulfill his needs? In what ways does this question reflect your life?

2. Read Psalm 17, noting the last two verses in particular. How can the psalmist approach God with such certainty that he will be satisfied? Do you have the same comfort? Why or why not?

2

AFFIRM THAT APPETITES ARE A GOOD THING

Only God can fully satisfy the hungry heart of man.
Hugh Black

"In the beginning God created . . ." These first words of the creation story give us a glimpse into what God really had in mind when He created the world. The Bible tells us six times that God looked at what He had made and said that it was "good" (Genesis 1:4, 10, 12, 18, 21, 25). But after He made man, God said that it was "very good" (1:31).

It is important to recognize the place of appetites in the creation. Man and woman, with all their individual appetites, were created before sin entered the world. As Adam and Eve were created good, so also were their appetites. They had no need to focus on selfish fulfillment because they were in close communion with God.

Our loss of that primary communion made us lose control of our appetites. Blame this revolutionary event on the Fall, the event that changed everything for the worse. Our appetites themselves are not sinful—after all, God gave them to us—but we sometimes choose to satisfy these appetites in a sinful way. However, when we satisfy our appetites according to how He intended them to be fulfilled, we are acting just as God designed us.

Your Appetites are "Very Good" by Design

What's so "very good" about our appetites as God designed them? Here are several answers.

Appetites provide foundational motivation. At their core, appetites serve the basic purpose of motivating us to live life to the fullest. It is through our appetites for having, doing, and being more than we are that we act to improve our current situations.

Appetites draw people together. If not for the appetite to have companionship, humans would not hunger to be with other people. This appetite fuels a desire for intimacy, taps into our sexuality, and ultimately leads us to procreation.

Appetites sustain us physically. Food is necessary for energy and survival; therefore, God made us want to eat. He also made it possible for us to truly find pleasure as we enjoy the food He provides.

Appetites lead us to pleasures that enrich and fulfill. Feelings of pleasure, whether physical or spiritual, are a gift from God (1 Timothy 6:17). Provided an appetite is being satisfied in a way that honors God, the pleasure that follows is God-ordained.

Appetites can stimulate a sense of adventure and push us outside of our comfort zone. Our appetites cause us to search for what is new and exciting. Traveling the world, playing the violin, or taking up surfing are all life-enriching activities that were likely started with an appetite for the unknown.

Appetites draw us closer to God. We have within us a longing for a relationship with our Creator. To want to know God is a quality that has been imprinted on each one of us. Our desire for spiritual security leads us to seek our heavenly Father. When we do so, we find peace and joy and love in abundance.

Eight Appetites "In the Beginning"

There are eight appetites covered in the first three chapters of Genesis. As you study the beginnings of these appetites, consider carefully whether you might be struggling with any of them.

1. The Appetite for Food. The appetite for food is revealed in Genesis 1:29: "Then God said, 'I give you every seed-bearing plant on the face of the whole earth and every tree that has fruit with seed in it. They will be yours for food'" (see also Genesis 2:16). God provided food for Adam and Eve and told them what they could eat because they needed to eat food. God also placed restrictions on what they could eat: ". . . but you must not eat from the tree of the knowledge of good and evil" (v. 17).

To eat and to feast is a common theme in the Bible. God created His people to love to eat, and He encouraged them to feast as a means of celebrating the blessings He gave them throughout the year.

2. The Appetite for Sex. The appetite for sex is revealed in Genesis 1:28: "God blessed them and said to them, 'Be fruitful and increase in number; fill the earth.'" Procreation was something God commanded Adam and Eve to do. But this was no ordinary command entailing duty or work, and God didn't give it to men and women just because it would populate the world. Look at what Scripture says just before the command to "be fruitful": "God blessed them." The gift of sexual union was a blessing from God, not just a command. God blessed Adam and Eve by giving them an appetite for the pleasure of their sexual union and for becoming "one flesh" (Genesis 2:24).

3. The Appetite for Authority and Power. The appetite for authority and power appears in Genesis 1:26: "Then God said, 'Let us make man in our image, in our likeness, and let them rule over the fish of the sea and the birds of the air, over the livestock, over all the earth, and over all the creatures that move along the ground'" (see also verse 28). God created man to be in authority over the rest of God's creation. As a result, the appetite to have authority is understandable.

The appetite for authority and power did not end the day we got kicked out of the Garden. Some of the best examples of God continuing to direct people to use this appetite in a healthy way are presented in the

New Testament. Jesus gave His disciples authority over demons (Luke 10:19–20), not for selfish ends but for God's purpose, to carry out His will as it is revealed to us. Jesus also gave His disciples authority to use His name to heal people (Acts 3:6-8). As believers today, we have been given the same authority through the power of Jesus' name.

4. The Appetite for Pleasure. This appetite becomes obvious when we read Genesis 2:9: "And the Lord God made all kinds of trees grow out of the ground—trees that were pleasing to the eye and good for food." God created the world, and specifically the Garden of Eden, to be pleasing to the eye. God created us with five senses through which to enjoy the things He made, and He gave us the appetite to experience pleasure through these senses. God made everything for us to enjoy (1 Timothy 6:17).

5. The Appetite for Work. The appetite for work can be seen in Genesis 2:15: "The Lord God took the man and put him in the Garden of Eden to work it and take care of it." When God created man, He did so with some very specific plans and purposes. As we know, when God has a plan, He creates within us everything we will need to accomplish that plan. Since God intended for Adam and Eve to take care of the Garden, He created them not only with appropriate skill and talents, but He also caused them to desire to do so. So from the very beginning, we were created with an appetite to work.

6. The Appetite for Companionship. The appetite for companionship is recorded in Genesis 2:18: "The Lord God said, 'It is not good for the man to be alone. I will make a helper suitable for him" (see also verses 20 and 24). The need to be with other people, to love and be loved, and to feel a sense of acceptance and belonging is at the very core of every human being. Our appetite for companionship and love is a healthy, God-given desire. We are made in God's image, and God desires companionship with us (Psalm 135:4; Zechariah 2:10; Titus 2:14). We were created for His pleasure. Since God takes pleasure in us (Psalm 149:4; Zephaniah 3:17), it is only natural that we would desire time together with each other.

7. The Appetite for Fellowship with God. In the beginning, God and humans had direct and personal fellowship together in the Garden of Eden. Throughout the first few chapters of Genesis, we see God's interactions with Adam and Eve. They spoke directly to each other. God gave instructions (Genesis 1:29–30; 2:15–17) and also blessings (1:28). Adam chose names for each of the animals God created (2:19–20). They spent enough time together for God to know that Adam was missing something he needed (a suitable helper). They worked together to fix that problem (2:18–25).

Adam and Eve apparently fellowshipped with God often enough to know the sound of His footsteps. We know this because in Genesis 3:8, after they had sinned, Adam and Eve "heard the sound of the Lord God as he was walking in the garden in the cool of the day." That sounds like a pretty close relationship, doesn't it?

Today, our appetite for fellowship with God continues (Psalm 27:4; 84:2), and He continues to call us to fellowship with Him. First Corinthians 1:9 says, "God, who has called you into fellowship with his Son Jesus Christ our Lord, is faithful."

The evidence is substantial and clear that we have been created with an appetite for God that can be satisfied by nothing other than God. Happily, God desires to be with us and claims us as His own: "Know that the Lord is God. It is he who made us, and we are his; we are his people, the sheep of his pasture" (Psalm 100:3). Enjoying fellowship with God is our deepest longing and our most precious treasure. It is this appetite that, when filled, will keep all our other appetites in their proper order and priority. We must learn to fill this appetite first and foremost if we hope to fill the other appetites.

8. The Appetite for Gaining Wisdom. This appetite is mentioned in Genesis 3:6, just moments before sin entered the world. "When the woman saw that the fruit of the tree was . . . also desirable for gaining wisdom, she took some and ate it." Eve had an appetite to gain wisdom that drew her closer to this deadly fruit. Having the desire to gain wisdom is not wrong. Like the other appetites, it was something God created us to have.

Jesus is described as growing in wisdom (Luke 2:52). The book of Proverbs was written for the purpose of attaining wisdom. Solomon was greatly loved by God because he favored wisdom over all other earthly pursuits. As God's children, we too must seek wisdom, since it is a gift from God.

Just as the world and our first parents were created good and beautiful and in communion with God, so too were our appetites. Understandably, the greatest hunger we will ever have is our appetite for fellowship with God. What a joy to know that we can be satisfied spiritually and have a committed relationship with our heavenly Father.

As we travel this road to regain control of our appetites, we can be encouraged to know that all our appetites are subject to God's authority. The question of how to satisfy our appetites becomes instead a call to seek to obey God in all circumstances and through all appetites and desires. That means making the necessary choices to satisfy our appetites in a manner than honors Him. When we do, true fulfillment is our reward.

A MOMENT TO REFLECT

1. Did any of the eight appetites' beginnings noted in this chapter surprise you in any way? If so, how? Which of these eight appetites would you consider to be "problem" appetites for you? Why?

2. Read Ecclesiastes 2:24–26. Does this passage make you feel uncomfortable? Why or why not?

3

AVOID SUBSTITUTES FOR WHAT YOU REALLY WANT

For when I am weak, then I am strong.
The Apostle Paul
2 Corinthians 12:10

As we have learned, our appetites are God-given and serve beneficial purposes in our lives. If our appetites are God-given and beneficial, you might ask, what's wrong with satisfying them? In truth, there isn't anything wrong with satisfying them. The danger is in seeking to fill an appetite with something that doesn't belong there. We may be using the wrong things altogether or using the right things in excess or in the wrong way. But most often, we attempt to use one appetite to fill another one.

Appetites are best satisfied with the actual substance desired. Yet we often don't fill our appetites with what they desire or what we really need. Instead, we attempt to make substitutes for the real needs and experience pain every single day. Attempting to fill an appetite with something that doesn't fit causes our appetites to become unhealthy and dangerous.

It isn't hard to see how something of great value can become something utterly destructive. Consider the element of fire. Fire enables us to keep warm, heat up food, and light up the darkness. But the benefits of fire are appreciated only when a blaze is controlled and contained. If a fire is left to feed itself or moves outside its boundaries, it can cause incredible ruin and even be life-threatening. Uncontrolled fire is capable of devouring everything in its path.

An appetite is like a fire. Under control it helps a person survive, but out of control it destroys everything in its path, including the person. An appetite out of control can destroy intimacy, scorch our freedom, and char our relationship with God. The longer an appetite blazes out of control, the more difficult it is to bring back under control. Yet such a task is never impossible.

Beware of the Power of the Flesh

So many things changed once sin entered the world. When Eve took the fruit, ate it, and then gave some to Adam, their desire to please themselves exceeded their desire to please God. From that moment on, this has been our biggest struggle: the battle between flesh and spirit, man and God, self and others, wrong and right. It's a battle we fight every single day.

Because of the Fall, we are born into a sinful world with a sinful nature that wants to do nothing but satisfy its selfish desires. Our flesh wants to feel good no matter what the cost. And it's not content to feel good eventually. No, we want pleasure and we want it now! Our sinful nature demands immediate gratification and the bigger the pleasure, the better. Since the Fall, we have to struggle with the reality that many of our appetites run contrary to the will of God and must be controlled or they will control us.

Although Satan had a hand in twisting what God created to be good into something bad, he didn't do it alone, and he doesn't do it alone today. Satan is only responsible for providing the temptation; the choice is still up to us. Satan tempts us with the things our sinful nature already desires. But there are times when we choose to sin without Satan helping us at all. Sometimes our flesh wants something, and we decide to give in. We often don't need much persuasion.

David Sper writes in *Designed for Desire*, "The root of all sexual perversions and immorality begins with the desire to relieve one's pain with pleasure."[a] As humans, our main goal seems to be to seek pleasure and avoid pain. So when pain is experienced as a result of our inability to satisfy our cravings, we continue to seek bigger and bigger pleasures to override and hopefully erase our pain.

Every sin is the result of an appetite going astray and being filled by something other than what God intended it to be filled with. We experience the appetite through the sensation that something is missing inside. Then we begin looking outside of ourselves to fill it. This can become especially destructive when what we need is something spiritual and yet we are looking to the physical world to fill it. We must learn instead to seek a spiritual relationship with God to fill ourselves first.

Otherwise, we will seek to fill ourselves with something God didn't plan, and we will find ourselves in the middle of sin. Harry Schaumburg writes, "When people seek a taste of heaven by their own means, they create a living hell of uncontrollable desires."[b]

We so often want to believe that the reason our appetites get out of control is that we are feeling deprived or are missing something that we think we really need. We may say, "If I just had enough money to pay my bills, I wouldn't need to drink the way I do." Or, "If I had someone to love me, I wouldn't need to be looking at this pornography." But the reality is that no matter how much we have, we are not spared from the possibility of our appetites getting out of control. No matter how much you love God, you are not exempt from temptation. We turn whatever we believe is missing into an excuse for our poor choices.

Can You Spot a Fake When You See One?

When we rationally consider that what we really want and need is a close relationship with our Creator, it seems ridiculous to think that anything on this earth could even come close to imitating our spiritual desires. Surely nothing this physical world has to offer could begin to fill our spiritual longing. But Satan is a clever enemy, and we should never underestimate him. Satan knows we have a passion for worship, and he has come up with several imitations that can easily fool the unsuspecting eye. Consider drugs and alcohol as Satan's substitutes for religion and worship, and see how they measure up. Both can:

- provide immediate but temporary answers to the problems of boredom, rejection, loneliness, depression, and anxiety;

- offer the possibility of unity and connection with other people through gathering together and socializing;

- offer at least temporary relief from the pain of internal conflicts;

- erase disappointments, frustrations, failures, and feelings of inadequacy;

- produce feelings of self-confidence, self-assurance, and internal strength;

- provide us a haven of comfort, rest, and peace from the chaotic world.[c]

Satan's choices are not so far off from what we are seeking. That's why we can be so easily persuaded to settle for less. We become convinced that this immediate option is "close enough." Jeff Vanvonderen, in his book *Good News for the Chemically Dependent and Those Who Love Them*, states, "The real danger with chemicals is not that they don't work. The real problem is that they do, at least while the effects of the chemical are present."[d] He raises two major concerns regarding the working of chemicals in a person's life:

1. Chemicals are sometimes more dependable than people when it comes to helping with emotional pain.

2. Chemicals cause additional problems and pain, but, at the same time, they are capable of numbing the pain that should be signaling that there's a problem.[e]

If you are not capable of spotting Satan's substitutes for God's abundant life, then you are in danger of falling into his snares. When God offers you peace, joy, and fulfillment, He delivers exactly what He says. However, when Satan presents you with one of his substitutes, he doesn't tell you the whole story. Remember, Satan is the father of all lies. He tells just enough of the truth to get you interested and then leaves the rest out, and lies by omission are still lies.

Look at what Satan tells Eve in the Garden of Eden, as presented in Genesis 3:1–5. Satan asked Eve a question as an attempt to make her doubt what she knew. "Did God really say, 'You must not eat from any tree in the garden'?" When Eve answered that she knew what God had instructed—that if they ate of the tree in the middle of the garden they would die—Satan started his deception. He presented some truth and left off the rest. "'You will not surely die,'" the serpent said to the woman. "'For God knows that when you eat of it your eyes will be opened, and you will be like God, knowing good and evil.'"

Satan told only part of what would happen if Eve ate the fruit. More accurately, he told only the immediate benefits to Eve. He skipped telling her the rest of the story. He didn't explain to Eve that when she ate of the tree and had her eyes opened to know good and evil, she would also:

- feel guilt and shame,
- have her relationship with her husband negatively affected,
- be embarrassed by her nakedness,
- never again have the same relationship with God,
- experience fear,
- go through the pain of childbirth, and
- die.

Why doesn't Satan tell the whole story? Because he knows that if we see how things will really end up, we won't want what he's offering. This technique doesn't only work for Satan. Advertisers and marketing firms the world over now regularly use this strategy to sell their products. Replay in your head the last TV commercial you saw for beer. Only one side of the story is given to the consumer watching the ad, right? We watch the poolside scene and think, Yes, that is the life . . . having a nice, cold beer and being with friends, all of us gathered around the barbecue. That's the way I want to enjoy myself this weekend.

Have you ever seen an alcohol commercial showing a drunken man abusing his wife? Or the funeral of a teen killed by a drunk driver? Or the aftermath of an alcoholic mother whose children were removed from her home because she wasn't properly caring for them? Such somber ads would tell the whole story of what alcohol is capable of when overindulged.

Christians need to be vigilant when it comes to hearing the truth. Were we to examine carefully the real story behind how our choices to fulfill our appetites affect others, we wouldn't likely give in to our fleeting desires quite so easily by making the wrong choice.

A MOMENT TO REFLECT

1. Study James 1:12–15. Describe this process in regard to a recent instance with your problem appetite, tracing the initial desire, an enticement, and eventually a sinful result. What awaits the Christian who fights temptation?

2. Find three Scriptures that speak to a believer's need for self-control and the reward for reining in unhealthy desires. Consider memorizing at least one of them.

4

JUMPSTART THE CHANGE PROCESS

Private victories precede public victories.
You can't invert that process any more than you
can harvest a crop before you plant it.
Stephen Covey

Only the very naive Christian believes that our struggle with sin stops at the point of salvation. If anything, our struggle with sin starts at salvation. Why? Because before salvation we don't struggle with sin—we just give in to it. We are slaves to our controlling sinful nature. It is not until we become a part of God's team that the real struggle with our old team begins.

You soon realize that old habits die hard. You know that you are loved and accepted by your new Coach, Jesus, but your old teammates of lust, greed, pride, and envy keep calling you and trying to convince you to return to them. What are you going to do? You reluctantly decide to go to your Coach and tell Him about it. When you do, you are surprised to find out He already knew all about it. He tells you that this happens to every member of His team. The most important thing Jesus tells you is that there is hope!

Peace is not out of reach, and neither is mastery of our appetites. Healing begins with the resolution of our inner conflict between the body and the spirit. As the body gravitates toward comforts and sensual pleasures, the spirit desires meaning, permanence, and truth. The tug-of-war at times feels like it could rip us apart, but it is part of the Christian walk and cannot be traded or circumvented.

Knowing that control of your appetites is possible though Christ's power and presence, you can launch into the process of change with confidence. Here are some key first steps.

Seek Forgiveness from God and from Yourself

We are not made acceptable before God as a result of our own merit. Only through His grace, forgiveness, and unconditional love are we made clean. And only by acknowledging our need for forgiveness and being willing to give and receive forgiveness do we have a chance at the healing we so desperately need.

If we do not deal with the issue of forgiveness, we will continue to hold on to negative emotions such as hatred, anger, bitterness, and resentment. We must acknowledge that we have these feelings toward ourselves, toward others, and possibly toward God before we will begin to control our appetites. Without forgiveness, we will be headed right back into using our appetites to medicate the pain we are experiencing.

We start by admitting that we need to be forgiven. In order to see your need for forgiveness, you will have to face the reality of how you behaved and whom you have hurt. If we refuse to admit what we have done wrong, we are not ready to begin healing. But when we admit and confess our sins, God does an amazing thing: He forgives us and makes us clean (1 John 1:8–10).

We need to confess that we have allowed our appetites to become idols to us. We have sought immediate gratification through the things of this world, at times to the point of harming our body, which is the temple of the Holy Spirit (1 Corinthians 6:19). And we have negatively affected our witness for Christ through our lack of self-control. We must confess all of these things to God and seek His forgiveness if we are going to begin to live victoriously.

After confessing to God and receiving His forgiveness, the next step in the forgiveness process is seeking forgiveness in your relationships with others. Giving and receiving forgiveness are closely tied to each other. As a matter of fact, we can't have one without the other (Matthew 6:14–15). We must follow the example set for us: "Bear with each other and forgive whatever grievances you may have against one another. Forgive as the Lord forgave you" (Colossians 3:13). If we have any hope of being forgiven ourselves, we must learn to forgive others.

We may need to seek the forgiveness of others for hurts we have caused, for not loving as we were called to love, for not letting our life be a witness for Christ to them, and for directly sinning against them. Asking for forgiveness means we should be willing to make restitution where necessary. Ask God to guide you as you approach these people and the pain both you and they may feel. We must be willing to face the pain once and for all, to walk back through the heartache if necessary to grieve over it, admit it, accept it, and forgive it.

The final step of forgiveness involves being willing to forgive yourself for the mistakes you have made. This may be the toughest facet of the whole concept of forgiveness. We continue to beat ourselves up emotionally and mentally for the mistakes we have made and confessed to God. When we do, we are in a sense telling God that we don't really believe He has forgiven us. Dwelling on your confessed past mistakes is not part of God's plan for your life. So if you find yourself haunted by your past, remember it is not God reminding you, because He has already forgotten it (Psalm 103:12). Satan wants to keep your past in front of you as a means of keeping you from experiencing the abundant life God promises to His children.

Take Responsibility for Yourself

If you hope to make peace with your appetites, you must realize that you are responsible for yourself, your choices, the consequences of those choices, and seeking the help necessary to change. Any change must be made by you accomplished through the power of the Holy Spirit in your life. Here are several ways to step up to the plate.

Stop Blaming Everyone Else! It is time to stop blaming the grocery stores and restaurants for our obesity, the tobacco industry for our lung cancer, the pharmaceutical companies and breweries for our chemical abuse, the casinos for our gambling addiction, the shopping malls for our compulsive spending, or the condom manufacturers for our teen pregnancies and STDs. If we hold any hope of healing, we must start putting the blame where it belongs—on each of us who refuses to control ourselves and our appetites.

Stop Making Excuses! Excuses are the rationalizations we use to help us feel less guilty about doing what we want to do. When our beliefs and behaviors are in conflict with each other, eventually one or the other will have to change. Unfortunately, what often changes are our beliefs, not our behaviors. Getting real with ourselves means we must decide to base our beliefs once and for all on God's Word and stop making excuses for behaviors that fall outside those boundaries. The only healthy way to resolve the conflict between our beliefs and our behaviors is to start changing our behaviors to act in accordance with God's will for our lives, because that never changes.

Stop Believing Your Own Lies! We use everything imaginable to lie to ourselves and avoid having to make the needed changes. Christians have even used their Christianity as one of their excuses: "I'm already forgiven"; "God loves me no matter what I do"; "God made me this way, so I know He understands"; "There is no condemnation in Christ, so I don't have to feel bad about this." But being Christian does not mean that we have freedom to do whatever we want just because we know we are forgiven. We should never use our freedom as a Christian to rationalize our continuing experience in the appetites of the flesh. We must stop lying to ourselves and stop abusing our freedom in Christ if we are to be healed.

Nurture Healthy Relationships

God desires that we live in community, and His plan for

restoration includes other people becoming connected to us. Our interaction with others satisfies some very basic needs, such as our need to be loved and accepted just as we are. God not only created these needs in us, He also provided the means to meet those needs through our healthy relationship with our biological family and our church family.

Another benefit healthy friends and companions afford us is that they can provide us with encouragement and accountability during our struggle to bring our appetites under control. Spending time with family and friends who hold similar beliefs and values will help us to stand strong in our personal choices. The battle to control our appetites is easier when others care enough about us to check on us, encourage us, lift us up, and hold us accountable.

Another way to meet our need for nurturing is through participating in various types of groups. Whether it's a Bible study, support group, therapy group, or any variety of club or organization, getting involved with others can help us feel like we belong. As we become more comfortable with people in these groups, a sense of closeness can develop that allows us to share areas of concern and places where we could use some extra support and nurturing.

Find Your Purpose

Our appetites tend to get out of control when we focus on them and our need to fulfill them. So how do we avoid falling into the trap of becoming self-absorbed? By having a purpose actively centered in others instead of ourselves. Having a purpose means asking what we can do for the greater good of mankind or maybe just the little old lady down the street.

Our purpose is how we contribute to society in a positive way and make a difference in someone's life. When we become focused on others more than on ourselves, we begin to feel satisfied on the inside. Filling up on healthy things gets us to the point of being able to make peace with our appetites and stop them from raging out of control in an effort to fill us up some other way.

As we search and find our purpose in life, we will find that our self-esteem starts to improve and life begins to have true meaning. No longer merely surviving day to day, we can start living the abundant life God intended us to live—free of controlling appetites.

A MOMENT TO REFLECT

1. Define "forgiveness." Read Psalm 130. Do you feel uplifted and encouraged? Why or why not?

2. What steps will you take in your efforts to remove temptation from your life and actively seek change? Write out a purpose statement for your life as you begin anew.

5

BE AWARE OF APPETITE TRIGGERS

Never think we have a due knowledge of ourselves till we have been exposed to various kinds of temptations, and tried on every side. This thought should keep us humble. We are sinners, but we do not know how great. He alone knows who died for our sins.
John Henry Newman

Our appetites for food, sex, power, companionship, and so on do not race out of control or find a healthy balance in a vacuum. Let's take a look at the major factors that can influence our appetites either positively or negatively.

Biological and Physiological Influences

The importance of the brain in influencing our appetites cannot be underestimated. As the communication center to your nerve cells, the brain is the basis behind everything you think, feel, and do. It is the brain's job to constantly monitor what is going on in the body and to seek a state of internal "balance." It does this through the use of brain chemicals called neurotransmitters which gather information about what's going on in our body and signal the best way to respond. For example, when you place your hand on a hot stove, the nerves in your hand communicate to the brain through neurotransmitters that there is danger and something hurts. The brain instantly communicates through neurotransmitters to tell the muscles of the arm and hand to retract from the pain.

The two neurotransmitters identified and most studied are serotonin and dopamine. When released into the brain, these substances bring about feelings of calmness, happiness, peace, and satisfaction and can increase mental awareness and alertness. The desire to experience the feelings produced by serotonin and dopamine can become a craving or a compulsive demand—a runaway appetite.

Substances that seem to increase the amounts of these chemicals include carbohydrate-rich foods, antidepressants, alcohol, drugs such as cocaine, heroin, and stimulants, chocolate, and sunshine and light. Activities associated with the increase of these neurotransmitters include feeling loved, exercise, sex, acts of benevolence and love, and the experience of beauty and art. Things associated with lowering the levels of these chemicals, which in essence will cause us not to experience pleasure, include stress, low self-esteem, hormonal adjustments, high-protein diets, too little sunlight for extended periods of time, and an absence of love.

In addition to serotonin and dopamine, other body and brain chemicals also influence our appetites.

Hormones. Insulin is a hormone that triggers hunger and is closely related to blood-sugar levels. As blood-sugar levels decrease, insulin levels increase and motivate us to eat. Once eating has started, the opposite reaction occurs. As blood-sugar levels begin to rise, insulin production is decreased and the desire for food intake is terminated. Research has shown that obese people tend to have chronically high levels of insulin in their bodies, thereby causing a persistent sense of hunger.

Leptin is another hormone that influences our appetite.

It has been shown to decrease the rewarding value of food and increase the rewarding value of activities that are incompatible with eating. This new research shows great potential for aiding the fight against obesity.[f]

Endorphins. Endorphins are powerful natural opiates responsible for producing feelings of intense pleasure and for reducing and relieving pain. Foods with a high-fat, high-sugar combination, as well as alcohol, have been shown to increase the production of endorphins. Endorphins are also released in response to highly palatable foods and have been shown to cause a response in the brain similar to morphine. Like the neurotransmitters discussed above, anything that will cause these natural opiates to be released will likely become something we desire and crave.

The "runner's high" is a result of the release of endorphins in the brain. This grueling act of self-discipline rewards with a sense of well-being that is experienced through endorphin release. This is one reason so many people seem to become addicted to exercise. There would likely be many more couch potatoes who refused to get their bodies moving if not for the emotional changes and mood alteration endorphins bring.

Cultural Influences and Pressures

Many of our so-called natural appetites are being created, shaped, twisted, and distorted through the constant infiltration of the media in our culture. What we once would never have considered, we eventually begin to believe we "need" in order to survive or be acceptable. Each of us can come up with at least one (if not many) things we have bought or seriously considered trying that we never would have otherwise considered had it not been the advertising campaign or media from which we learned of the product.

A person with a sex drive that is difficult to control is going to be more frustrated after seeing sensual images on television. A person with a food problem will find their control weakening if they don't use discretion about how much and what type of television they watch. And anyone with a disposition tipped toward materialism will most likely want more when the advertisers tout products consumers "cannot live without."

Peer Pressure

We are relational beings by nature, and as such we have an innate need to experience a sense of acceptance and belonging. Our strong need to "fit in" can drive us to give in to the mighty power of peer pressure. The belief that "everyone is doing it" has a tremendous pull on what a person who isn't participating can convince himself he really wants and needs.

Consider the college freshman who never had an appetite for alcohol through high school because she was surrounded by strong Christian friends who desired to not drink. But when she moves away to start college, she looks for a new set of friends who will accept her. The first time she refuses a beer at a party and gets teased and ridiculed for it will be the last time because she wants to be a part of the group. Peer pressure has created in her an appetite for alcohol. And peer pressure can create an appetite for just about anything for someone who needs to "fit in."

Social Cues

Social cues are as powerful on our appetites as are biological cues. We eat because it is time to eat or because someone brought a cake to work or because we are bored. We crave certain foods not based on what our body is telling us it needs for nourishment, but because it is a specific holiday or social event. Responding to our appetites in general is triggered more by social habit than anything else.

Cornbread stuffing is a case in point for me (Steve). A single tablespoon of stuffing probably contains three grams of fat, but at Thanksgiving and Christmas I don't care. I just can't stop eating it. My craving for stuffing can be traced back to my childhood when pleasurable family dinners created warm memories and feelings that increase my appetite beyond control during the holidays.

Childhood Abuse or Neglect

Some appetites that have reached the addictive state can be caused by an early childhood trauma or a sense of rejection. Children's needs and desires start out innocent and appropriate. But when abuse, neglect, or other serious family dysfunction is present in a child's life, her appetites may become twisted and harmful to herself and others around her.

The extended deprivation of basic needs or the presence of intense and extensive negative attention causes children to experience a sense of emptiness that runs deeper than many of us can ever know. Rejection early in life can leave a person with an almost insatiable thirst for approval.[g] This emptiness and longing may drive an abused child to seek fulfillment from a variety of unhealthy sources.

Some studies estimate that as many as 80 percent of sex addicts may have been abused in childhood. Often the victim grows up to be the victimizer, practicing the behaviors he learned from a parent or other significant adult. The susceptibility to other addictions, such as alcohol and drug abuse and gambling, are often linked at least in part to unmet childhood needs.

Parental Influences and Learning

As we grow up, we are constantly learning from the people around us. Our parents, siblings, caregivers, and teachers all affect our learned patterns and behaviors. When we watch a stressed parent turn to the refrigerator, the television, the weight bench, or the cigarettes for relief, we believe that those are effective ways of making us feel better when we are stressed. We also may witness adults using food, alcohol, or relationships as a means of rewarding themselves for some accomplishment or other activity.

Either way, we are learning from their examples that such behaviors can bring instant feelings of pleasure and relief and serve as a fix for whatever the situation is. We imprint these "solutions" and are very likely to experiment with them and respond in a similar manner when we begin to experience our own stress and tension levels increasing.

Psychological Influences

Our emotional state can play a huge part in our appetites and how we choose to respond to them. It is a well-known fact that stress, depression, and anxiety all affect the various chemicals in the brain that work to regulate our moods. For example, there are multiple appetite-related symptoms that may indicate depression: changes in appetite (regarding food), a lack of motivation, a loss of the sense of pleasure in all or most activities, feelings of worthlessness, a decreased libido.[h]

Even more common is the existence of stress. It seems our society thrives on stress and keeps pushing us harder and harder to do more and more. Unfortunately, when our bodies are experiencing stress, it is the brain's job to reinstate balance. So the more chronic your level of stress, the more you will find yourself searching for something to bring pleasure and therefore balance to your life.

False Beliefs Tied to Identity and Self-Worth

People who are struggling with low self-esteem and a low sense of self-worth are held prisoner by a set of irrational and false beliefs as to who they really are. Regardless of what may have caused them (childhood experiences, rejections, losses, etc.), these false beliefs can drive people into an ever-increasing spiral of negative thoughts that may become a set of self-fulfilling prophecies. These strongly held beliefs could push their appetites out of control and actually confirm (at least in their own mind) that what they believe is true.

When we accept a set of false beliefs, they will become the driving force behind our choices, our appetites, and our lives. Before our appetites can begin to change, we will have to face the reality of the beliefs we have been holding and come to an understanding of who we really are in Christ.

Clinical Addiction

A behavior is potentially addictive in the clinical sense if:

- it takes more and more time and keeps you from filling your obligations;
- it continues in situations that are physically dangerous;
- it causes repeated legal or social problems;
- it has come to replace other important activities;
- it causes bad physical or emotional feelings if stopped;
- it needs more of something to get the same effect and is impossible to stop.

Even after reading this list, you may be unsure whether you have a clinical addiction. It is very difficult for an individual to objectively evaluate his situation. Addictions may be subconscious and are often kept secret because of shame or guilt. They can arise slowly or quickly. They may even have short-term positive benefit that masks their potential danger. There are also different styles of addiction. If you are unclear whether you are struggling with clinical addiction, seek out a professional opinion.

Relationship Patterns

Interpersonal relationships are one of the main ways we go about getting many of our emotional and psychological needs met. We are relational beings, and we each have a strong need to be loved and accepted. Our desire for companionship is from God and runs very deep into the core of who we are.

This powerful drive to avoid loneliness in our life can cause us to seek out and hold onto relationships at all costs. This can result in a person choosing to remain in unhealthy, destructive relationships. When relationships do break up, our appetite for companionship will intensify and drive us to find another relationship that we hope will fill us up and keep us full.

Spiritual Influences

"For the sinful nature desires what is contrary to the Spirit, and the Spirit what is contrary to the sinful nature . . . so that you do not do what you want" (Galatians 5:17). This is the dilemma that, unfortunately, all of us live with. Desiring what is not beneficial to us leads to potentially addictive behavior. Our natural desires grow out of control, and we crave what is of the world and not beneficial to the soul. The desires that rage within us are obviously influenced by the spiritual world.

The presence of the Holy Spirit in our lives will call us toward a set of appetites that are wholesome and edifying. Galatians 5:16 says, "Live by the Spirit, and you will not gratify the desires of the sinful nature." The more we grow in our relationship with God, the more we will find ourselves hungering and thirsting after righteousness—and being drawn to appetites that really fill us up.

However, the Holy Spirit is not the only spiritual influence hoping to impact our appetites. Satan "prowls around like a roaring lion looking for someone to devour"

(1 Peter 5:8). One way he "devours" is by tempting us to give in to the desires of the flesh and the things of this world that he controls. Satan doesn't simply want us to partake in the things of this world; he wants us to binge on them. Although the devil cannot actually make us do anything, he is the master deceiver and has at his disposal the power to tempt us.

We can gradually become deceived to the point of deciding that whatever it is we want really is OK for us to indulge in. And that's just the first step. Satan wants us to take healthy appetites and make them our obsessions. He wants to then take our obsessions and make them addictions. And once there is an addiction, he wants to use it to completely control and destroy our lives.

Our innate rebelliousness against God couples with the many factors that influence our various appetites in the wrong direction. Intentionally or unintentionally, you have trained your brain to crave the specific things it does. Your brain now needs to be retrained. Let us reflect on the hope-filled words of Jesus in Mark 10:27 as we continue the journey: "With man this is impossible, but not with God; all things are possible with God."

A MOMENT TO REFLECT

1. Name three influences from this chapter you can relate to in your own appetite battle. Describe how each influence has affected your thought process as you fight temptation.

2. Read Romans 8:5–27 and meditate on the miracle of a life lived in the Spirit. Do you rejoice with Paul in his declaration? How will this passage help you when the next battle comes?

6

FIND SATISFACTION IN ALL THE RIGHT PLACES

When Christ reveals Himself there is satisfaction in the slenderest portion, and without Christ there is emptiness in the greatest fullness.
Alexander Grosse

God wants us to be fulfilled and satisfied. He wants us to be successful in controlling our appetites and meeting our needs without excess. And we can be satisfied, if we faithfully commit to follow His leading. Keep this truth in mind as we delve into the eight appetites outlined in chapter 2.

1. The Appetite for Fellowship with God

When God created us, He left a place inside us empty and yearning to be filled with the love and fellowship of our

Creator. By doing this, God created a need for Himself. This desire should drive us toward a relationship with the Almighty that will make us whole. Unfortunately, before many people find God, they find substitutes to fill that God-given void as best they can. As Christians, we know intellectually that this won't work, but that doesn't stop us from trying.

Until we seek, find, and accept a relationship with God, we will long to fill that space and probably have our passions stirred by something else. Romans 1:18–31 tells us that God makes Himself known to men. However, "although they knew God, they neither glorified him as God nor gave thanks to him, but their thinking became futile and their foolish hearts were darkened. . . . They exchanged the truth of God for a lie, and worshiped and served created things rather than the Creator" (vv. 21, 25).

When we attempt to put anything in the place that only God is to fill, we are committing the sin of idolatry. Are you seeking things and experiences as a substitute for God? If so, you are deeply entrenched in the sin of idolatry and need to put God back in His place of priority. If you don't, you will continue to seek the things of this world to fill your appetite for God and you will continue to feel empty.

2. The Appetite for Pleasure

Other than our desire for God, the appetite for pleasure is the creed by which we as human beings live. We want to experience a sense of pleasure and avoid pain in everything we think, feel, and do. We want our relationships, our jobs, our recreation, our food, and even our death to be pleasurable. We want to live in an enchanted world where everything is rosy and beautiful and where we never want for anything.

In reality, we know that this is an impossible dream, but it is still what we hope for. But when we experience pain, we immediately begin searching for something to relieve the pain and restore the pleasure. The deeper the perceived pain, the stronger is our felt need for release through some form of pleasure. Eventually, normal pleasures no longer do the trick, and "forbidden" pleasures seem necessary to escape the pain. We must fill our appetite for pleasure God's way (Psalm 16:11).

3. The Appetite for Food

People today use food as a way to escape pain in their lives. They may feel emotional pain from a relationship breakup, psychological pain from depression or anxiety, or any one of countless other pains. When the appetite for food careens out of control, it can threaten just about every aspect of our lives.

Eating when we are not hungry can still cause the brain to release chemicals that bring about intense feelings of pleasure. So if you are stressed and use food as your medication, you really may feel better, at least for a while. But then the pain comes back. And this time it brings along feelings of guilt and shame from eating when you didn't really need to. And how will you get rid of these painful feelings? You will probably take more "medicine."

No matter how hard we try, we cannot fill our spiritual or emotional needs with physical food. The Bible tells us our appetite for food will never be satisfied: "All man's efforts are for his mouth, yet his appetite is never satisfied" (Ecclesiastes 6:7).

4. The Appetite for Sex

God created sex to be pleasurable. And because He did, He also had to give many commandments and instructions regarding it. God knew how easily this appetite could become distorted and destructive. But because of our sinful nature, many people are drawn into sins of sexual immorality. The result is a whole series of sexually related consequences, such as STDs, AIDS, teen pregnancies, abortions, unwed mothers, and broken marriages. Sexual addictions, lust, pornography, homosexuality, and prostitution are all related to our feeble attempts to make ourselves happy by perverting the blessing of sex that God provided us with. Ecclesiastes teaches that sexual gratification can become a snare with chains worse even than death (7:25–26). To experience the fulfillment God designed, we must keep our sexual appetite within the bounds of purity and obedience to God's Word.

5. The Appetite for Authority and Power

We live in a power-hungry society. This drive for power and authority can become all-consuming for some people. While they are climbing their way to the top, they don't seem to care who they walk over. The only reason they even want other people around is to use them as stepping stones to move themselves closer to the peak.

When the appetite for power gets out of control, people will begin to use their position to get what they want. They become consumers of people instead of consumers of things. The lives of the people around such power mongers come under the jurisdiction of this self-proclaimed god. Ecclesiastes says this control and extortion of others will eventually only bring the one in power more hurt and pain (Ecclesiastes 7:7; 8:9). In contrast, Jesus said that filling the appetite for power and greatness comes through being the servant of all (Matthew 23:11–12).

6. The Appetite for Work

The problem isn't your willingness to work hard; it's working hard for the wrong reasons that causes this appetite to rage out of control. When you work compulsively for the purpose of fulfilling your desire for pride, power, or possessions, then it's time to reconsider what life is really all about (See Ecclesiastes 2:18–23).

It is good to be willing to work for your keep and to stay busy. Proverbs 10:4 tells us, "Lazy hands make a man poor, but diligent hands bring wealth" (See also 12:24, 19:15, 21:25–26, 24:30–34, and 2 Thessalonians 3:10). But God never expected us to become workaholics. God rested on the seventh day (Genesis 2:2). We too are commanded to not work on the Sabbath (Exodus 20:8–11). Jesus took time to rest while here on earth, even though He knew He had only three years to change the world (Mark 4:38, 6:31; and John 4:6).

Are you using work as a way to fill yourself up on the inside? Have you determined that your sense of worth and value depend on your job performance? Do you find your sense of security being tied to money, career, or other things that work gathers for you? If you find yourself answering yes to any of these questions, then it's likely that work has become your god.

7. The Appetite for Companionship

We have been created with a strong need and desire for relationships with other people. In the New Testament, we are told not to forsake the assembling together of believers (Hebrews 10:25). God knew that we would want to be around people; and if we don't choose to be around other believers, who will we choose to be with? Obviously, nonbelievers. There are several times in the Old Testament where God instructs the people of Israel to avoid spending too much time with pagans because He knew how easily they could be drawn away from Him.

Our appetite for companionship can become destructive as a result of our choices of the people we surround ourselves with. Because of our strong need to belong and feel accepted, choosing to spend time with unhealthy people will eventually begin to influence our thoughts, beliefs, and actions. We will start to be more like them and doing the same types of things they do. This is the power of peer pressure at work.

8. The Appetite for Wisdom

There is nothing wrong with knowledge and wisdom or the desire to attain them. Only when our desire to gain wisdom reaches the point of overindulgence, obsession, or misdirection should we become concerned. When our desire to pursue wisdom is stronger than our desire to pursue the One who gives wisdom, then knowledge has become our god.

Let's again turn to the teachings of Scripture in the book of Ecclesiastes:

- "For with much wisdom comes much sorrow; the more knowledge, the more grief" (1:18).
- "Do not be overrighteous, neither be over wise" (7:16).
- "Of making many books there is no end, and much study wearies the body" (12:12).

These verses show that an excessive desire for knowledge can bring problems. Overindulgence in the study of anything, even religious topics, can distract us from the really important issues. Second Timothy 3 says that in the last days, people will have "a form of godliness but denying its power . . . always learning but never able to acknowledge the truth" (vv. 5, 7). In today's world with all the information you could ever imagine right at your fingertips through the Internet, our appetite for wisdom can be even more difficult to control. But it must be managed and controlled and used only for purposes that would be pleasing to God.

Now that we have studied these eight appetites in detail, it is time to turn our attention to the healing process. God's desire for us to be in control of our appetites is real and powerful, and we may find healing if we seek to do His will, utilizing the good gifts He has given us.

— A MOMENT TO REFLECT —

1. The prophet Jeremiah speaks of a satisfied God-appetite. Read and meditate on Jeremiah 15:16. How would you assess your appetite for God and His Word?

2. Study the following Scriptures: Matthew 5:6; Luke 6:21; Revelation 7:15–17. What promises does God make to His children concerning their appetites?

7

EMBRACE A NEW POWER SOURCE FOR LIFE

God's power under us, in us, surging through us,
is exactly what turns dependence into unforgettable
experiences of completeness.
Bruce Wilkinson

As Christians, we have a secret weapon for dealing with our appetites: The power of the Holy Spirit living within us. When Jesus was leaving this earth, He promised to send the Holy Spirit to help His disciples and us (John 14:26). Through the presence of the Holy Spirit we receive wisdom, encouragement, power, and strength to help us as we battle (Acts 1:8; Acts 9:31; Ephesians 1:17). When we face trials and difficulties in our lives, Jesus tells us that the Holy Spirit is there to help us know how to handle the situation (Mark 13:11; Luke 12:11–12).

As the Holy Spirit lives and grows in us, we begin to produce good fruit as described in Galatians 5:22: "love, joy, peace, patience, kindness, goodness, faithfulness, gentleness and self-control." The fruit that grows from a plant reflects the source itself. Apples grow from apple trees, not tomato bushes. In the same way, the fruit that comes from the Holy Spirit in our lives will reflect its source: God Himself within us. It is only as we allow the Spirit to produce His fruit in our lives that we are able to take control of controlling appetites.

Forbidden Fruit from the Enemy

Satan uses forbidden fruit to entice us away from God and His provisions for our life. We can choose to pursue Satan's forbidden fruit instead of God's fruit, but we need to be aware that there are consequences to doing so, such as its effect on our physical bodies, our relationships, our finances, etc. Choosing to partake of forbidden fruit can also have consequences in the spiritual realm: Sin separates us from God, sin leads to spiritual death, and sin affects our witness to others for Christ.

God placed the choice of obedience or rebellion before Adam and Eve in the Garden of Eden, and He places the same choice before us every day. Not only does He give us the choice, but He also shows us plainly what the right choice is through His Word and the leading of His Spirit within us. Yet, just like Adam and Eve, we often make the wrong choice.

The substitutes that Satan offers may initially look similar to the spiritual fruit we know we need. He doesn't get us to indulge in his substitutes by only offering rotten, sour-tasting fruit. He offers fruit that tastes, looks, and in all senses of the word is "good." But what happens if you get involved in something "good" that isn't what you are supposed to be doing? If it's not God's plan for you, then you could be following Satan's substitutes and allowing him to pull you away from what God has in store for you.

You may want to evaluate yourself and your activities and see who you are following. Are you relying on your self-effort and sense of independence? Are you refusing to ask for help from your spiritual brothers and sisters because you need to look strong? Are you serving God with the wrong motives? Any of these can be substitutes that Satan is offering you. They look good on the surface, but their ultimate purpose is to draw you away from God and into disobedience.

What Fruit Are You Filling Up On?

When we are growing spiritually, the fruit of the Spirit is very appealing to us. When we are filling up with the fruit of the Spirit, we have much less desire to partake of forbidden fruit. However, when we are not filling our appetite with what the Spirit has to offer, we still have an appetite, and forbidden fruit begins to look more and more appealing. And when we are filling up on forbidden fruit, we will experience less desire for the fruit of the Spirit.

Satan's job is to tempt us to fill up on forbidden fruit instead of the fruit of the Spirit. Our job is to stand firm against these temptations and to resist him. Satan doesn't tempt us where we have no appetite. Instead, he hits us where we already experience some desire, want, or appetite. He starts with little thoughts at first that we allow ourselves to entertain as "innocent." And before long, the desire grows so big within us that all Satan has to do is stand back and give a little nudge to cause us to completely crumble.

Satan tempted Jesus in the areas of human appetite. First, after Jesus had fasted for forty days, Satan hit Him with the temptation for food (Matthew 4:2–3). Can you imagine just how deprived and hungry Jesus must have felt by the time Satan showed up? Because Jesus was totally man and totally God, He had the same physical needs and desires that we have. Any human body that has gone without food for forty days and nights is going to experience an extremely strong craving for food. But instead of giving into His physical needs, Jesus held His spiritual needs of pleasing God as more important.

Second, Satan presented Jesus with a temptation regarding the appetite for prestige by challenging Him to jump off the temple so the angels could rescue Him in front of everyone watching (Matthew 4:5–6). We all want to be a "somebody," and how better to prove that you are a "somebody" than to have ten thousand angels come soaring in to rescue you? But that was not a part of God's plan and was therefore a temptation that Jesus had to resist, which He did without denying who He is.

Finally, Satan tempted Jesus with two of the most powerful human appetites, offering power and possessions if Jesus would worship him (Matthew 4:8–9). By offering Jesus all the kingdoms of the world, Satan presented Jesus with the opportunity to exert His power and authority here on earth. Jesus had to resist the temptation of what looked good and to remember that God's plan is the only way to go.

Satan also presented Jesus with the opportunity for possessions. This is an area where many of us have a very soft spot. Satan offered Jesus not only the kingdoms of the world, but also their splendor. Remember, Jesus was human and had the desires that humans have, one of which is often the desire to acquire. But Jesus knew that acquiring possessions Satan's way was not the will of God, and He therefore resisted the temptation and commanded Satan to leave His presence.

When you look at these temptations, you can't help but notice a glaring fault in Satan's strategy—a fault that shows how we, too, can have victory over the temptations that confront us. Satan tempted Jesus with things He already had. All Satan's temptations did was to try to get Jesus to experience these things off schedule, at a time that would not honor God. So it is with us. God will give us the desires of our hearts—but not right now, not when we demand them, and not in the form we think they should come in. If we get off God's timetable by impulsively gratifying our desires, then we will never experience God meeting our need and providing abundance in our lives. So when temptation comes, don't think about having to have satisfaction now. Think about the honor of God giving you the desires of your heart in His own time.

Surrender and Respond to God's Spirit

Before we yield to God's authority, we do everything under our own power. And our power, which could not prevent us from losing control in the first place, cannot take back control now. Your only hope is to find victory by surrendering your life to God. Admit to God that the problem grew out of control under your own power. Believe that God cares about you and will fill you with His power and change your life through that power. Then allow God to do it.

Surrender to God is the beginning to healing. Surrender means that you no longer try to face the problem alone. In God's power and with the encouragement of fellow strugglers, you can go an hour or a day or a week at a time without responding to your appetite. Surrender to God means giving up and giving in, not to defeat, but to a new way of living that can lead to the satisfaction of all your appetites. God cannot fight this battle for you. He will stand beside you, providing you with all you need to win hands down. But it is up to you to use what He offers and to fight the fight.

As we begin to fight the battle with our appetites, we will soon see that we have three choices as to how we respond to temptation.

First, we can respond through our fleshly self that focuses on fulfilling our fleshly desires through immediate gratification and impulsiveness. Our fleshly self is driven to act out of simple reflex and is focused on self-fulfillment and pleasure.

Second, we can respond through our rationalizing self, which provides excuses and explanations that may alter reality in our minds in order to make our choice more acceptable to us. Our rationalizing self is more concerned with the reactions of others and the personal consequences we may experience as a result of our choices.

Finally, we can respond through our Spirit-controlled self, which involves seeking God's solution to the problem or temptation and doing what He would have us do. Our Spirit-controlled self seeks God's will regardless of the consequences.

If you are going to be victorious over your appetites, you must not respond to impulses as your fleshly self would have you do. And you must stop attempting to alter reality through excuses or explanations as your rationalizing self would have you do. You must learn to live under the Holy Spirit's control, doing first and foremost what God would have you to do.

A MOMENT TO REFLECT

1. Read John 15:1–8. According to this passage, how can we bear fruit? Read Galatians 5:16–17. What is God's remedy for victory over temptation to satisfy appetites Satan's way?

2. We can respond to Satan's forbidden fruit by appealing to our physical, rational, or spiritual nature. When faced with your problem appetite, which is your initial response? Explain.

8

WORK TOWARD HEALTHY BALANCE

The possibilities are numerous once
we decide to act and not react.
George Bernard Shaw

Learning to bring your appetites, and indeed your whole life, under control requires that you understand the concepts of balance and moderation. The Bible tells us, "The man who fears God will avoid all extremes" (Ecclesiastes 7:18). Life is like a teeter-totter with moderation being the pivotal point of balance in the center. The opposite ends of this teeter-totter are the extremes of total restriction and excessive indulgence. Living at either extreme is a life out of balance.

Total Restriction. Total restriction from healthy appetites, such as our appetite for food, is the wrong way to achieve balance in life. For example, almost everyone has at one point said "never again" to some kind of food, such as high-fat or high-calorie foods, sugars, or carbohydrates. But diet plans taken to this extreme produce negative consequences. Totally restricting your consumption of a particular food group can deplete your body of needed nutrients and result in physical damage.

Another negative consequence of total restriction, including food, is developing a sense of deprivation that may lead to stronger cravings for the desired substance. When someone becomes emotionally and spiritually weakened through restriction, Satan has a foothold for tempting them. It is more likely that this person will eventually indulge in the desired substance and possibly binge on it.

Some persons may need to classify a food or activity as "total restriction" due to health problems, addiction, or family history. But in general, our God-given desires were intended to bring us pleasure and to be experienced in moderation rather than eliminated entirely.

Excessive Indulgence. At the other end of the teeter-totter is excessive indulgence. Excess is defined as an "action that goes beyond a reasonable limit. An amount greater than is necessary."[i] Our motto in America seems to be "the more, the better"—no matter what it's more of. Just look at some of these statistics:

- Obesity rates have reached an all-time high of more than 30 percent of adults.[j]
- One out of five Americans has a sexually transmitted disease.[k]
- Television viewing has now reached 3 to 5 hours per day, depending on age.[l]
- Addictions now affect an astonishing 30 percent of American families.[m]
- Personal bankruptcies filed in 2001 numbered 1,452,030.[n]
- The average household has 16.7 credit cards with credit-card balances averaging almost $9,000 per household.[o]
- Consumer credit has reached an all-time high of over 19 percent of personal income.[p]
- There are now more registered cars on the road than there are licensed drivers.[q]

The problem isn't the enjoyment of pleasure through indulging; it is when our seeking of pleasure is unrestrained to the point that we forget all else and are no longer concerned about the consequences—at least for the moment. A life of excessive indulgence is a life full of sin. God speaks often about partaking in activities according to His rules and with moderation and self-control. There is no activity, substance, or desire on this earth that cannot become sinful when engaged in to excess. Reason is no longer in control; therefore, our desire to consume controls us.

Tips for Bringing Balance to Appetites

How do we go about managing the appetites we will inevitably encounter? This list of skills and suggestions has been collected from a variety of sources, with a few additions of our own.[r]

Practice Moderation. Moderation is, of course, the best strategy for taking control of the appetites that control you. Moderately indulging your appetite before it grows too strong will help you avoid overindulging. For example, you may want to allow yourself to watch one hour of television and then turn it off instead of sitting in front of it all evening. Or if you can't bear substituting celery sticks for ice cream, limit yourself to a small bowl instead of eating the entire half gallon.

Use Self-Talk. Learning to use self-talk can greatly improve your success in fighting your problem appetites. Get mad at unhealthy or inappropriate cravings. Instead of getting mad at yourself for giving into the craving, get mad before you over indulge. Direct your anger at the source instead of at yourself. When you succeed at controlling an unruly appetite, give yourself a pat on the back for a job well done.

Practice Thought Stopping. Thought stopping is the process of learning to take control of what you are thinking. As soon as you identify a thought as something negative or detrimental, you simply say "stop" in your mind or out loud (2 Corinthians 10:5). Then you replace the unhealthy thought with something healthier: a memory verse, your favorite praise and worship chorus, a pleasant childhood memory, plans for your next vacation, and so on.

Pamper Yourself. If the activity you have been

engaging in for pleasure is something that you now wish to manage or control, what better way to do so than with something else you enjoy? To do this, replace your out-of-control activity with anything else that brings you a sense of pleasure and that is not harmful to you or those around you.

Distract or Delay the Decision. Most appetites last only a few minutes. So delay your decision to act on a potentially harmful desire for fifteen to thirty minutes and then see if you really still want it. Sometimes we just can't outwait our appetites, so as long as they are not destructive, indulging with moderation is the right thing to do.

Engage in Self-Monitoring. Controlling our appetites has everything to do with getting to know ourselves better. Ask yourself what you are feeling before you indulge in a craving. Cravings often mask some negative emotion that you would just as soon not experience. This may be anger, depression, anxiety, boredom, loneliness, or a host of other emotions. Once you have identified the feeling behind the drive, you can more appropriately express or deal with your feelings, instead of simply trying to ignore it by engaging in some appetite that you believe will make the negative feeling disappear.

Fellowship with God. As we spend time with our heavenly Father, we gain wisdom and understanding and we grow stronger spiritually, thus more able to utilize the resources He makes available to us. Through this growth, we will better understand and use the weapons He gives us to fight the good fight and to stand firm against temptation.

Healthy Alternatives for the Unhealthy Appetite

Each of these alternative activities is a healthy means of satisfying natural desires by building us up and bringing us pleasure. Just remember that moderation is the goal in all activities.

Move your body. Exercise reduces stress, controls appetite, increases energy and body temperature, releases endorphins, and improves sleep quality.

Listen to music. When you need to relax, listen to calming music. When you need extra energy, listen to upbeat music that makes you want to move.

Get a massage. Massage creates a state of relaxation

and peace, decreases stress and anxiety, reduces blood pressure, and improves self-esteem with pampering and human touch.

Take a bath. Go the extra mile and make it a bubble bath or use some aromatherapy. A warm, soothing bath will produce feelings of relaxation and pleasure.

Read. Whether it's a good book, an inspirational story, or the sports section, find something to read that brings you pleasure and enjoy it as often as you can.

Get some R&R. Find fun ways to rest and relax, including getaways and vacations that last for a couple of days or more.

Pray and meditate on Scripture. Spending time alone in prayer and meditating on God's Word helps us remember who we are and how very much we are loved.

Talk to a friend or therapist. Talking through your problems with a close confidant helps relieve stress and helps you feel connected to another person.

Keep a journal. Spend time alone with your thoughts and feelings and then write about what's going on in your life and how you feel about things. When you put your feelings in writing, they become easier to understand and control.

Practice deep breathing. Effective deep breathing must come from the diaphragm. You will know you are breathing right when your stomach expands instead of your chest.

Become involved in discipleship. Discipleship involves growing in the wisdom and knowledge of God with other believers. Discipleship promotes spiritual growth and the relational connection and belonging we all need.

Do something for someone else. As you give yourself to others, you begin to realize that you are useful and have something to offer to others. You begin to feel more valuable—thus enhancing your own self-esteem.

Laugh. Laughter is good medicine, especially when it comes to managing stress and increasing pleasure in life. The more you can include laughter in your life, the better you will feel physically and emotionally.

Find a hobby. If you don't already have a hobby, find one. If you do have one, make time to do it on a regular basis.

Attend a meeting. Search out a recovery or support group that focuses on your problem appetite. Meeting others who are struggling and hearing how God is working in their lives will help you believe He is also working in your life.

A MOMENT TO REFLECT

1. Is seeking pleasure through indulgence wrong? Why or why not?

2. List three new methods or alternative activities from this chapter you intend to try to restore balance in your life.

⑨

CULTIVATE A DIVINE APPETITE

*The heart that has no agenda but God's
is the heart at leisure from itself.*
Elisabeth Elliot

God is the key to any success you may gain in learning to control your appetites. He needs to be your energy source, your pilot, and most of all your cornerstone if you want to become a new creature. God needs to be the force behind all you do, the one directing and in control of where you are headed, the foundation upon which you build your life.

Why is God so important? Because He is life! Jesus says in John 11:25–26, "I am the resurrection and the life. He who believes in me will live, even though he dies; and whoever lives and believes in me will never die." And in John 15:5 Jesus describes Himself as the Vine with us growing out of Him as branches. Through Him flows life, and apart from Him we can do nothing. Jesus is the most important part of anything and everything you do, think, feel, and say.

Charles Allen writes in *God's Psychiatry* that "we are created incomplete . . . and we cannot be at rest until there's a satisfaction of our deepest hunger . . . the yearning of our souls."[5] What does your soul yearn for? What is it that will finally bring you rest? The answer is found in Scripture:

- "My soul yearns, even faints, for the courts of the Lord; my heart and my flesh cry out for the living God." Psalm 84:2

- "My soul finds rest in God alone." Psalm 62:1

- "As the deer pants for streams of water, so my soul pants for you, O God." Psalm 42:1

- "Whoever drinks the water I give him will never thirst. Indeed, the water I give him will become in him a spring of water welling up to eternal life." John 4:14

- "I am the bread of life. He who comes to me will never go hungry, and he who believes in me will never be thirsty." John 6:35

This deepest craving we have is for God, our Creator. This craving can only be filled through a personal relationship with Jesus Christ and through the spiritual food and drink He offers.

Seek God First

When earthly things instead of God come first on our list of priorities, we are never satisfied and therefore never get to anything else on the list. And the more earthly priorities scream to be filled, the more they drown out the Holy Spirit beckoning us to Him. These out-of-control appetites begin to rob us of life and fellowship with God. And when that happens, our strongest need of all, our need for God, goes unfulfilled and our inner void grows bigger and more painful.

But there is hope! If we will fill our appetite for God first and foremost, all our other needs and appetites will be fulfilled.

Unlike our physical appetite for food, we can never really get enough of God. Physical hunger signals us to eat, and when we do, we are satisfied. But when our appetite for God is satisfied, it is also intensified. He fills us up, yet we want more of Him. Matthew 5:6 says, "Blessed are those who hunger and thirst for righteousness, for they will be filled." There is a blessing connected to this craving for God. If you have never actively sought out ways to feed your appetite for God, you may not realize how this appetite will develop.

Pursue the following activities with great energy, even if you don't really feel like it. There may not be immediate, tangible results. But God is faithful to His children, and our efforts to know Him more will not go unnoticed.

Study God's Word

Through our study and knowledge of the Scripture, we can:

- Know God better (Ephesians 1:17–18)
- Gain wisdom and understanding (Psalm 119:130–33; Philippians 1:9–10)
- Avoid stumbling spiritually by resisting temptation and sin (Psalm 119:9–16)

- Find hope (Romans 15:4)
- Mature as Christians (Ephesians 4:13)
- Gain prosperity and success (Joshua 1:8)

The Bible is our map or instruction manual to godliness (Psalm 119:105), and we need to read it often. Otherwise we will be walking in darkness and will surely stumble and fall. Just as you need physical food each and every day to sustain your body, you also need spiritual food every day to sustain your soul. We need to feast on God's Word daily as the psalmist did (Psalm 119:103).

Delight in the Lord

Scripture tells us to "delight . . . in the Lord and he will give you the desires of your heart" (Psalm 37:4). Do you know what spending time with God does to us? It changes us from the inside out. Through delighting in the Lord, we become new creatures with new hearts filled with new desires that God promises to richly fulfill. And that's how we mature as Christians. We draw closer to God and become more like Him, desiring the very things He desires for us.

What does it mean to delight in the Lord? Let's consider what it would mean if you had a friend you delighted in. What would that look like? You would spend time with her, talk often together, and look forward to your time together as you let her into your life and your world. That is exactly how we can delight in God. Through our reading of His Word, our prayers and meditation, and our worship of Him, we build a relationship with God in which we delight in Him.

Believe His Promises

From the first page to the last, Scripture is filled with the promises God has made to us. He loves us and wants wonderful things for us, yet we struggle to believe that God will really do what He says He will do. As we cultivate our divine appetites, we should take great comfort from His promises. Here are just a few of them:

- He is always near and will never forsake you (Psalm 37:28).

- He watches over you and cares for you (Psalm 121:3–8).

- He has good plans for you (Jeremiah 29:11).

- He will listen when you pray and seek Him (Jeremiah 29:12–13).

- He will give you strength (Psalm 68:35).

- He will forgive you when you fail (Micah 7:18).

Experience Fellowship with the Body

God encourages us through Scripture to spend time together with other believers (Hebrews 10:24–25). As you seek to grow closer to God and to feed your divine appetite, we encourage you to find a local church that you are comfortable with and start spending time with those people, growing healthy relationships that will in turn grow you.

There are several reasons that God encourages us to spend time together.

First, He provides us with friends and family who believe and behave in similar ways to help fill our need to be with people. These meaningful, healthy, and wholesome relationships are the ones we develop with other believers.

Second, our relationships with other believers also serve as a basis for support. Scripture says, "Carry each other's burdens, and in this way you will fulfill the law of Christ" (Galatians 6:2). Scripture also addresses sharing our joy with each other (Romans 12:15). It's been said that fellowshipping together divides the sorrows and multiplies the joys. What a wonderful thing God has provided for us through our spiritual family.

Third, being in close contact with other believers brings many opportunities to encourage each other (Hebrews 3:13). We can't encourage each other if we don't take the time to get to know each other in such a way that we feel comfortable sharing our needs.

Fourth, experiencing God's people will also help us as we grow spiritually through the process of accountability. Knowing that someone is going to check on us and ask us if we are doing what we need to be doing will remind us that we are loved and cared for. It is difficult to move too far away from God's plan when we feel accountable.

Finally, 1 John 4:11–12 says: "Dear friends, since God so loved us, we also ought to love one another. No one has ever seen God; but if we love one another, God lives in us and his love is made complete in us." Through our love for one another, we demonstrate Christ's love to the world around us.

Share in His Work

Growing closer to God includes becoming interested in what God is interested in. God is in the "people business." Everything He does centers around people. He wants to support them, provide for them, bless them, protect them, love them, forgive them, and most of all bring them closer to Him. If we want to join God in His work, that is what we need to learn to do (John 15:12–15).

Jesus modeled for His disciples the importance of serving others by washing their feet in the upper room (John 13:1–17). Serving others is about focusing more on their needs than on your own. It's about putting them first. Anything you do for another person as an act of service is like serving Christ Himself (Matthew 25:35–40).

When we take the time to be a part of the work God is doing for the people of this world, we not only please God and help others feel better, we also help ourselves. Focusing attention on the needs of others will tend to make us feel more productive and will therefore increase our overall sense of self-worth. God's kingdom is full of such opportunities for service and ministry.

A MOMENT TO REFLECT

1. How big is your commitment to God? Make a list of the major activities you do during the week. Note which ones are done for you and which ones are done out of love and service to God. Are you happy with the results of this exercise? Why or why not?

2. Which of the elements for cultivating a divine appetite in this chapter do you most need to concentrate on? List two or three steps you will take to grow stronger in that area.

10
DISCOVER GOD'S BEST FOR YOUR LIFE

Keeping God on the throne of your heart
is a daily discipline and delight.
Jan Carlberg

As Christians we are taught to surrender ourselves to Christ, but we may not be taught how to do that. Webster's Dictionary describes surrender as "to give up possession of; to give oneself up."[t] We know there is surrender when we commit our lives to Christ. Yet living our lives in continual surrender is more than a one-time decision. It becomes a daily part of our existence and shapes our entire world-view.

A Christian believes that salvation (choosing to believe in and accept Jesus Christ as our personal Savior) is the essential element to eternal life in heaven. The Christian also believes that living a godly life here on earth requires a daily willingness to let go of anything that may be standing in the way of us and the Creator. It is inviting Jesus in and asking the Holy Spirit to guide our lives and empower us to make the right decisions no matter how tough they are. That's daily, moment-by-moment surrender.

Many Christians have chosen Jesus as their Savior and stopped there. But if we really want to live a life pleasing to God, and if we want to let the Holy Spirit work through us, we must take another step. We must make Jesus not just Savior but also Lord of our lives. What's the difference? Accepting Him as Savior means that we understand we are sinners and deserve death as a result of our sin. It involves accepting that Jesus made the ultimate sacrifice by dying on the cross to take away our sins. Through our belief in Him we gain eternal life.

But when we make Jesus the Lord of our life, we surrender our will, desires, plans, and possessions—everything we have—to Him. He gets all of us to do with as He sees fit. Making Jesus Lord means that we don't hold anything back from Him. We don't give Him part of us and hang on to the rest to do with as we choose. True surrender means trusting Him enough to let Him take over control of our lives. God is in the driver's seat and takes us where He wants, when He wants, and the way He wants. There is no backseat driving when we are truly surrendered.

"Surrender is admitting that we can't handle life without God. We stop pretending to be God, get off the throne of our lives, and let God rule. In short, surrender means to obey him. We come to God on his terms, accepting that he is God and that he can do with us whatever he wants; but trusting that because he is a God of love, whatever he wants to do with us will be for our ultimate good."[u]

Trust and Obey

"Trust and obey, for there's no other way to be happy in Jesus but to trust and obey." The words of that familiar hymn resound with the essential elements of surrender. We must learn to trust and obey God if we are going to surrender our lives to Him. "For it is God who works in you to will and to act according to his good purpose" (Philippians 2:13). If we don't trust that

God loves us and wants good things for us, we are not likely to surrender our will to Him. Studying Scripture and gaining understanding of who God really is will help us to better trust Him as we hand our lives over.

Can you imagine saying you were surrendered to someone but had no intention of actually obeying him? Let's look at what Jesus has to say about obedience:

If you love me, you will obey what I command. . . . Whoever has my commands and obeys them, he is the one who loves me. He who loves me will be loved by my Father, and I too will love him and show myself to him. . . . Jesus replied, "If anyone loves me, he will obey my teaching. My Father will love him, and we will come to him and make our home with him. He who does not love me will not obey my teaching. These words you hear are not my own; they belong to the Father who sent me. (John 14:15, 21, 23–24)

The importance of obeying God's commands is stated often in Scripture, and almost always the act of obedience is paired with a blessing of some sort or another (Leviticus 25:18; Deuteronomy 4:29–31; 6:3; Jeremiah 7:23). When we choose to do what God tells us to do, things will go well for us and God will bless us: "Blessed rather are those who hear the word of God and obey it" (Luke 11:28).

Success through the Spirit

Even after salvation and making the choice to surrender to Christ as Lord of our life, we will still face struggles and trials in regard to controlling our appetites. We tend to fall back easily into old patterns that are focused on our flesh instead of the Spirit that lives within us. The urges we faced before surrendering to Christ will still present themselves, at least for a while, but now we don't have to face this battle alone. The Holy Spirit is there to strengthen us.

There are times when these temptations will feel so strong we may say, "I can't make it through this one." And you may be right. But here's the hope: You don't have to. Once you have accepted Jesus as your Savior, He lives within you. According to Scripture, "I have been crucified with Christ and I no longer live, but Christ lives in me. The life I live in the body, I live by faith in the Son of God, who loved me and gave himself for me" (Galatians 2:20). If we have been crucified with Christ, we are dead to ourselves and what lives within us now is the Spirit of God.

Jesus Christ lives in us and promises to help us resist temptation and to strengthen us to surrender and do His will (1 Corinthians 10:13). The Lord will never ask you to do something you can't do. Why? Because if we truly have died to self and have Christ living within us, then it is really Him being asked to do whatever it is. Furthermore, we know we "can do everything through him who gives me strength" (Philippians 4:13). We can control our appetites. As you embark on this challenge to surrender, we recommend that you engage some outside help in the form of a trusted friend or professional counselor or a self-help or support group.

You must be willing to let go of control and to surrender to the help your counselor offers. Don't try to control the therapist, the direction of therapy, or even yourself. Control is an attempt to exert power, and real power comes from God. As you surrender to the treatment process and begin to work through your pain, you will find relief from the very pain that has held you hostage. Through the power of the Holy Spirit, you can begin to control yourself and your appetites. With increased self-control will come increased self-confidence and freedom from the need or desire to control others. Surrender yourself to God and take this step to healthy, victorious living.

Why not start today? What better time to start taking control of your appetites than right now? Your battle for control happens one day at a time and starts fresh each day. Don't look back at the time you have missed, and don't focus on how long it is going to take. Just do what you have committed to do each and every day and watch as God blesses your efforts.

Here are twelve steps to launch you into taking control. Start working on them today!

Twelve First Steps to Controlling what's Controlling You

1. Make a list of the areas where you are not demonstrating self-control. Consider all appetites, even if your struggle is only moderate. Don't get overwhelmed by this list—you are not going to try to fix them all at once. But the list will give you something to prioritize and start working on.

2. Make a list of the lies you have been telling yourself. What lies and excuses are you using to allow yourself to continue in an unhealthy pattern? Admit them and stop using them. Here are several examples:

- "I don't deserve to be loved."
- "I'll never amount to anything."
- "I'm damaged goods."
- "I really love him, so sex is OK."
- "I can stop this whenever I want to. I just don't want to."
- "Everyone's doing it."

3. Evaluate your self-talk. You need to become more aware of what you are saying to yourself because your self-talk can have a big influence on how you feel and act. If you are constantly cutting yourself down and criticizing yourself, either in your head or out loud to others, you will have difficulty liking yourself or believing that you are capable of successfully making the necessary changes. However, if you are positive about yourself and your ability to change, you are halfway there.

For example, if you find yourself saying something negative like, "It's hopeless. I'll never get this under control," write it down. Then find a healthier statement to replace it, such as, "I know if I really commit to this, I can make a change."

4. *Make a list of healthy activities that bring you pleasure.* Include the small day-to-day things that make you smile as well as bigger events you look forward to. The more items you can come up with the better. This list is going to help retrain your brain. The more you can engage in the things you enjoy that are healthy for you, the more your brain will push you to act on these activities in times of stress so that the old, unhealthy behaviors remain a thing of the past.

5. *Confess, repent, and seek.* Before you can grow spiritually, you must remove all barriers that stand between you and God. You must admit that you have been struggling with controlling your appetites and that

these activities may be sinful. As you identify these sins in your life, you must confess and repent (decide to stop doing it). Take time to seek the help of the Holy Spirit by asking for the strength and power necessary to make these changes.

6. Grow in wisdom, knowledge, and understanding. If you hope to become more Christlike, you must know what Christ is like. Study God's Word on a daily basis and do your best to commit portions of it to memory so you will have it readily available to you when temptations come. It is through God's Word that we gain an understanding of what He commands us to do, how the Holy Spirit works in our lives, and the promises God provides to us.

7. Draw closer to God. There are two major benefits to drawing closer to God. First, as we draw closer to God and get to know Him through spending time with Him, we will begin to see sin and the things of this world as they really are. Second, as we get to know and trust God more, we will notice that we are being transformed to a closer likeness of Him. Our desires will change to match what His desires are for us.

8. Engage in spiritual warfare. See the enemy for

who he is and fight him with the weapons you have been given. Stop being deceived either through temptations or by believing that you are powerless in this battle. Remember, you are a child of the King, and He has made everything available to you to succeed in this fight with the enemy.

9. Take control of your thoughts. The battle for control of your appetites begins in the mind. If you learn to control your thoughts, your battle can end right there. The problem most of us have in this area of thought control is that we don't catch our thoughts soon enough. Many thoughts that eventually turn negative may start out seemingly innocent. This is part of Satan's deception. If he can get us to entertain the little thoughts, then he can gradually grow them bigger and bigger right under our noses. Wrong thinking cannot lead to right doing. We must have right thinking if we want to engage in right doing.

10. Determine to work on one appetite at a time. One of the biggest culprits to being unsuccessful in making changes comes in the form of becoming overwhelmed. Pick one appetite where you would demonstrate more self-control and start there. Put any others you listed in the first exercise away, and don't start on them until you have achieved sufficient success on the one you chose.

11. Stop feeding your flesh. Make a plan of action as to how you will go about changing your behavior and fulfilling this appetite in a healthy way. Be sure that the goals you set are realistic and that you give yourself a sufficient amount of time to see change. Remember, you didn't get to this place overnight, and you won't get out of it that way either. Some psychological research has shown that it takes approximately twenty-one days to break an old habit and form a new one.[v] So be patient with yourself.

12. Discover your state when your appetite is under control. Look at your life. Examine yourself. Discover where you are in control of your longings and impulsive urges and reflect on how you feel. Determine to spread those feelings to all areas of your life.

A MOMENT TO REFLECT

1. Would you define your spiritual life as a "surrender"? Why or why not? What is holding you back from this necessary step?

2. Read James 1:2–4 and Romans 8:28. How has God used the problem appetite in your life to bring spiritual growth? How are you experiencing greater Christ-likeness as a result of this journey?

CONCLUSION
A Note to the Still-Frustrated

Now that you are nearing the end of the book you may feel frustrated because you did not have a life-changing experience while reading it. Perhaps walls didn't tumble down, lights didn't flash, and you still feel pretty much the same as when you started.

It's OK. You're in the majority because change doesn't usually come from simply reading a book. But this could be the beginning of changes that lead to a new life for you. It all begins with taking the first step. You have effectively done that by reading this book this far. If you try to implement some or all the twelve steps provided in chapter 10, the journey to fulfilling your appetites will continue. The implementation of one new change can create a momentum that will lead you to more changes.

If you are frustrated, view it as a really good sign. Frustration comes from being one way yet knowing there is another way, a better way. We hope this truly will be a new beginning for you. If the urge to do whatever you have been doing overwhelms you, please, get up and get out of the house. It doesn't matter whether you go to a meeting of friends, a support-group meeting, or merely to visit someone in need. If you can't get out of the house, pick up the phone and call a friend. Start that conversation with a simple admission of needing to talk, of needing some assurance.

This is how life change begins for most people. Over a long period of time, small changes lead you to connect to people in new, deeper, and richer ways. So if you are frustrated, move on and take a baby step into a new life.

If you need assistance in finding a Christian counselor or other resource in your area you can phone 1-800-NEW-LIFE anytime, night or day.

Please visit our Web sites at Newlife.com and LoseItForLife.com.

References

a. David Sper, ed. *Designed for Desire* (Grand Rapids, MI: RBC Minisries, 1993).

b. Harry W. Schaumburg, *False Intimacy: Understanding the Struggle of Sexual Addiction* (Colorado Springs, CO: NavPress, 1992), 60.

c. Stephen Apthorp, *Alcohol and Substance Abuse: A Clergy Handbook* (Wilton, CT: Morehouse-Barlow, 1985), 158-162.

d. Jeff Vanvonderen, *Good News for the Chemically Dependent and Those Who Love Them* (Minneapolis, MN: Bethany House Publishers, 1991), 40.

e. Ibid., 40-42.

f. Colette Dowling, *You Mean I Don't Have to Feel This Way?* (New York: Bantam Books, 1993), 88.

g. "Coping with Food Cravings" (July/August 1991); http://www.primusweb.com/fitnesspartner/library/nutrition/cravings.html.

h. *Diagnostic & Statistical Manual of Mental Disorders: Fourth Edition* (Washington, D.C.: American Psychiatric Association, 1994).

i. *Webster's New World Dictionary of the American Language*, ed. David Guralnik (New York: Warner Books, 1984), s.v. "Excess."

j. Neal Barnard, M.D., "Breaking the Food Seduction," *Good Medicine* 12, no. 3 (Summer 2003), n.a.

k. David Sper.

l. "Comparisons of U.S. and Finnish Television Statistics." See http://www.uta.fi/FAST/US2/NOTES/finstats.html.

m. "Are you addicted?" *USA Weekend* (September 26-28, 2003), n.a.

n. American Bankruptcy Institute, "U.S. Bankruptcy Filings 1980-2002." See http://www.abiworld.org.

o. Jean Sahadi, "Debt: How do You Stack Up?" *CNNMoney*. See http:money.cnn.com/2003/09/25/pf/millionaire/q_dedstackup/index.html.

p. Ibid.

q. Justin Lahart, "Spending Our Way to Disaster," *CNNMoney*. See http:money.cnn.com/2003/10/02/markets/consumerbubble/index.html.

r. *Stress Management for Dummies*, "Curbing Your Appetite for Stress-Inspired Eating." See http://cda.dummies.com/WileyCDA/DummiesArticle/id-973,subcat-EATING.html. "Controlling Appetite for Weight Loss." See http://jas.family.go.com. "When Stress Triggers Overeating." See http://www.24hourfitness.com. "Conquer Killer Cravings." See http://www.floridafitness.com/Fitness/Craving_killers.html. "Cravings, Overeating, and the Brain Connection." See http://www.thedietchannel.com/weightloss5.html. "Coping with Food Cravings" (July/August 1991). See http://www.primusweb.com/fitnesspartner/library/nutrition/cravings.html.

s. Charles Allen, *God's Psychiatry* (Ada, MI: Flemming Revell, 1988), n.a.

t. *Webster's New World Dictionary of the American Language*, ed. David Guralnik (New York: Warner Books, 1984), s.v. "Surrender."

u. Steven Arterburn and David Stoop, *Seven Keys to Spiritual Renewal* (Wheaton, IL: Tyndale House Publishers, 1988), 7-8.

v. "Practicing Self-Control." See http://www.personal-budget-planning-saving-money.com/selfcontrol.html.